DISCOVERING SCIENCE

SOUND

Rebecca Hunter

Raintree

www.raintreepublishers.co.uk
Visit our website to find out more information about **Raintree** books.

To order:
☎ Phone 44 (0) 1865 888112
🖹 Send a fax to 44 (0) 1865 314091
🖥 Visit the Raintree Bookshop at www.raintreepublishers.co.uk to browse our catalogue and order online.

First published in Great Britain by Raintree,
Halley Court, Jordan Hill, Oxford
OX2 8EJ, part of Harcourt Education.

Raintree is a registered trademark of Harcourt
Education Ltd.

Produced for Raintree by Discovery Books Ltd
Design: Ian Winton
Editorial: Rebecca Hunter
Consultant: Jeremy Bloomfield
Commissioned photography: Chris Fairclough
Illustrations: Keith Williams, Stefan Chabluk
and Jenny Mumford
Production: Jonathan Smith

Originated by Dot Gradations Ltd
Printed and bound in China by South China
Printing Company

ISBN 1 844 21571 7
07 06 05 04 03
10 9 8 7 6 5 4 3 2 1

British Library Cataloguing in Publication Data
Hunter, Rebecca
Sound. – (Discovering Science)
534

A full catalogue record for this book is available from the
British Library.

Acknowledgements
The publishers would like to thank the following for
permission to reproduce photographs:
Bruce Coleman: page **21** (Wayne Lankinen); Discovery
Picture Library: page **4**, **23** (bottom); Chris Fairclough:
page **8**; gettyimages: page **5** (Stewart Cohen), **6** top (H
Richard Johnston), bottom (Darrell Gulin), **7** (Peter
Correz), **13** (Roy Hamaguchi), **15** (Mary Kate Denny), **16**
top (Art Wolfe), bottom (Pal Hermansen), **17** (Darryl
Torckler), **20** (Paul Chesley), **22** top (Bruno De Hogues),
bottom (Robert Frerck), **23** (Louis Grandadam), **28** (Ian
Shaw), **29** bottom (Todd Powell); NASA: page **12**, **19**;
SES ASTRA: page **29** top.

Cover photograph of a trumpet reproduced with
permission of Getty Images.

The publishers would like to thank the following schools
for their help in providing equipment, models and
locations for photography sessions: Bedstone College,
Bucknell, Moor Park, Ludlow and Packwood Haugh,
Shrewsbury.

Every effort has been made to contact copyright holders
of any material reproduced in this book.
Any omissions will be rectified in subsequent printings if
notice is given to the publishers.

Any words appearing in the text in bold, **like this**, are explained in the Glossary.

CONTENTS

A WORLD OF SOUND

We live in a world full of sounds. Listen to the sounds around you now. If you are at home, you can probably hear people talking and the television or radio playing. If you are outside you may hear the sound of traffic moving, birds singing or dogs barking.

A busy street is full of unusual noises.

Even when you are somewhere quiet, like a library, you will hear sounds. People will be whispering, walking quietly or turning the pages of their books.

Sound is always present. It is very difficult to create total silence.

This peaceful early-morning scene looks as if it would be totally silent. In fact you would probably be able to hear the sound of birds and the rustle of the wind in the trees.

TYPES OF SOUNDS

Sound is a form of energy that we can hear. Some sounds occur naturally, others are made for a purpose. The wind rustling leaves in the trees or thunder during a storm are natural sounds.

The sound that waves make as they crash against the beach is a natural sound.

Living things growl, roar, sing and call to each other for many reasons.

This bird is singing to attract a mate.

A cat purrs to show others it is happy.

People speak and make noises to communicate their feelings. Think of the number of words we use to describe noises we make.

WHISPER
LAUGHING
Murmuring shOUT

SQUEALING

Many sounds are noises made by machines. These are often loud, annoying noises. Noisy machines can be a real nuisance to people.

SOUND WAVES

Have you ever lined up a row of dominoes and then knocked the first one over? The first one knocks over the second, which knocks over the third, and the whole line falls over in a wave. The dominoes fall as one domino passes its energy to the next. This is something like the way sound travels.

Everything, including air, is made up of tiny **particles**. These particles are so tiny that we cannot see them. When a sound is made, these particles **vibrate**, or move back and forth. As air particles vibrate, they bump into each other and pass on their energy. The moving particles of air pass on their vibrations in the form of a sound wave. Because air particles are all around us, the waves of sound do not travel only in straight lines like the dominoes. Sound waves travel outwards in all directions.

When this alarm clock rings it creates tiny waves in the air. We hear these waves as sound.

PROJECT

This homemade 'telephone' shows how sound travels as vibrations.

You will need:
2 paper cups
6 metres of string
a friend to help.

1. Make a hole in the bottom of each cup. Thread the ends of the string through each cup and tie a knot.

2. Get your friend to hold one cup while you hold the other.

3. Walk apart until the string is stretched tight.

4. Hold the cup to your ear while your friend talks into his or her cup.

You will hear your friend's voice because vibrations run along the string to your ear. What happens if a third person puts their finger on the string? This will prevent the vibrations being carried any further. Sound stops travelling along the rest of the string.

SPEED OF SOUND

Sound does not only travel through air. It can travel through all solids, liquids and gases, because each of these is made up of **particles**.

How fast sound travels depends on what it is travelling through. The closer together the particles, the faster sound travels. The particles in solids are much closer together than those in liquids or gases. So sound travels fastest through solids. Engineers who build tunnels tap out messages on metal pipes. They can 'talk' to each other in tunnels by using metal's ability to carry sound.

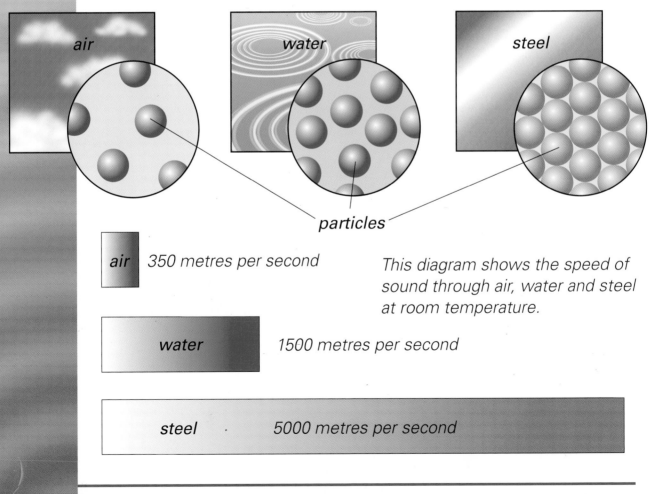

air

water

steel

particles

air — 350 metres per second

This diagram shows the speed of sound through air, water and steel at room temperature.

water — 1500 metres per second

steel — 5000 metres per second

PROJECT

This experiment shows how sound moves more easily through solids than air.

You will need:

a tuning fork (you may need to ask your music or science teacher for one of these)
a rubber
a wooden table
a metal pipe
a brick or tiled floor
a friend to help.

1. Ask your friend to strike the tuning fork on the rubber and hold it in the air 30 centimetres away from you.

2. Cup your hand round one ear and listen to the sound.

3. Now ask the friend to do the same thing, but this time touching the base of the tuning fork on the table well away from your ear. Listen to the sound through the table.

4. Repeat this experiment using the metal pipe and the floor at the same distance each time.

Which substance carries the sound of the tuning fork the best?

SOUND IN A VACUUM

A **vacuum** is a completely empty space. It contains no air and no other **particles**. Sound needs particles to move, so it cannot travel in a vacuum. In 1658, Irish scientist Robert Boyle did an experiment to prove this. He put a ticking watch in a glass jar and slowly pumped out the air until there was none left. When he did this, the sound of the ticking disappeared. This showed that sound cannot travel in a vacuum.

There is no air in space, so there are no sounds. Astronauts have to talk to each other using radios inside their helmets.

SOUND OR LIGHT, WHICH IS FASTER?

Think about being at a show with fireworks. Have you ever noticed how you see the fireworks explode before you hear them? The same thing often happens in thunderstorms. You see lightning before you hear the thunder, even though both happen together.

This is because sound travels more slowly than light. In 1 second, a beam of light travels very close to 300,000 kilometres (186,000 miles). In the same second, a sound wave travels only 320 metres.

You will always see fireworks just before you hear them.

HEARING SOUNDS

Three things are needed to make and hear a sound. The first is the thing that **vibrates**, or the source of the sound. The second is the medium – the solid, liquid or gas **particles** through which the sound will move. Finally, you need a receiver – the ear that hears the sound.

receiver

medium

source

Humans produce sounds by forcing air from their lungs past the vocal cords in their throats. The vocal cords produce vibrations that make the sound.

You can feel the vibrations if you place your fingertips against your throat when you speak.

HEARING

Sound waves are collected by the outer ear and directed into the middle ear. Here, three bones pass the sound waves to the inner ear. Then, the **fluid** in the spiral-shaped cochlea, sends messages through nerves to the brain. Finally, the messages are interpreted in the brain as sounds.

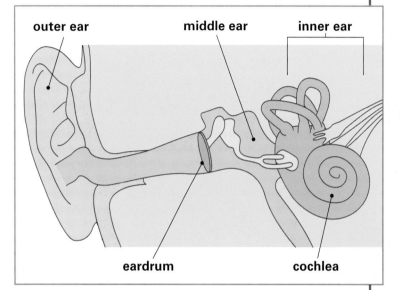

outer ear middle ear inner ear

eardrum cochlea

Deafness means a loss of hearing. This can be a total loss or a partial loss. There are many kinds of deafness and several ways of overcoming it. Many people who have poor hearing can be helped by wearing a **hearing aid** in the ear. The hearing aid magnifies the sounds, or makes them louder, so that they can be heard.

People who are totally deaf have developed another way of speaking. They use sign language. Sign language is filled with meaning. People use signs made with their hands to share their thoughts and ideas.

ANIMAL HEARING

Many animals depend on their sense of hearing to stay alive. These animals have large ears to help them hear the softest of sounds.

An elephant can hear sounds from many kilometres away.

Not all animals have ears that stick out from their bodies. A short-horned grasshopper's hearing organs, are found on the sides of its stomach. They are hidden under its wings. The long-horned grasshopper's hearing organ is on its front legs!

A grasshopper has ears on its body or legs!

You may think people can hear well, but almost all animals can hear better than we do. Dogs can hear sounds we cannot. Bats have even better hearing. They make very high-**pitched** squeaking sounds. These sounds bounce off objects and help them to locate their **prey**.

Dolphins and whales also use high-pitched sounds to communicate with each other as well as to find their food underwater.

VOLUME

The **volume** of a sound depends on the amount of energy the sound waves carry. A sound with a lot of energy is loud. Softer sounds have less energy.

Sound waves lose energy as they spread out through the air. Because of this, the closer you are to something, the louder it sounds. As you move away from the source of a sound, the sound energy is lost and the sound becomes softer.

We measure volume in **decibels** (dB). The loudness of a sound is measured on the decibel scale. The loudest sounds on this scale are more than 120 dB. Such sounds are very dangerous. No one should be exposed to these loud sounds without ear protection.

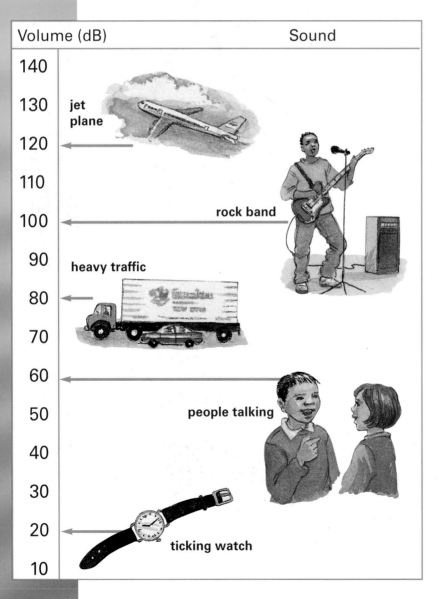

Volume (dB)	Sound
140	
130	jet plane
120	
110	
100	rock band
90	
80	heavy traffic
70	
60	
50	people talking
40	
30	
20	ticking watch
10	

An enormous amount of energy is needed to launch a space shuttle.
This energy comes from its fuel which is turned into movement energy,
heat, light and sound.

MUFFLING SOUNDS

When sounds are too loud, they can become annoying. If you are playing music in one room, people in the next room may not want to hear it. This is why walls in houses have **insulation**, a material that muffles the sound, in them. Car engines are also insulated so that people travelling in them do not hear all the noise from the engine. A sound insulator slows or prevents sound from passing through it. Some materials are better at muffling sounds than others.

Rock musicians who play music that is over 100 **decibels** often suffer hearing loss. You should remember this when playing music on a stereo at home. Headphones produce loud sounds, and almost all the sound goes directly into the ears. Listening to music like this for too long, can damage your hearing.

People who work in places with loud sounds should always wear ear protectors to muffle the sound or make it quieter.

PROJECT

You will need:

an alarm clock

some materials, such as newspaper, plastic packing material or sawdust and different types of fabric (for example towelling or wool)

a large box

a notebook and pencil

a tape measure

a friend to help.

1. Set the alarm clock to go off in a couple of minutes. Put it in the box and surround it with one of the materials. Seal the box. Ask your friend to stand by the box.

2. Walk about 18 metres from the box. Ask your friend to wave when the alarm clock goes off.

Walk slowly towards the box until you can hear the muffled ringing. Now measure the distance you are standing from the box.

3. Repeat the experiment using each of the different insulating materials.

4. Make a chart to show the distance measured for each material. The closer you can get to the box, the better insulator the material is.

Which material is the best sound insulator?

MUSICAL SOUNDS

Musical instruments make air **vibrate** in many different ways. One of the oldest musical instruments is a drum. A drum is made by stretching a tight skin across a frame. Hitting the skin makes it vibrate. A tightly-stretched skin makes a high sound, while a loose skin makes a lower sound.

These tambours, or drums, are being played in Burundi, Africa.

Wind instruments use air blown through pipes to make sounds. The simplest wind instrument is a set of pipes made of wood or bamboo. The pipes are different lengths. Short pipes make high-**pitched** notes, and long, larger pipes make low-pitched notes.

This girl from Ecuador is playing traditional pan pipes.

Brass instruments also involve blowing air through a pipe. The harder you blow, the louder the noise!

Players of stringed instruments make sounds using vibrating strings. How high or low a note is depends on the length and thickness of the string, and how tightly it is stretched. The strings are played with a bow or plucked by hand.

This brass instrument is a saxophone.

This boy is tuning his guitar. The more he tightens the string, the higher the note will be.

Wind, brass and stringed instruments are combined together in a group called an **orchestra**.

PROJECT

Make a drum.

You will need:

a large biscuit tin
something to make the skin:
a piece of leather or rubber
or a plastic bag
an elastic band or piece of
string
a stick, ruler or spoon.

1. Stretch the piece of leather, rubber or plastic over the tin and hold it in place with the elastic band or string.

2. Tap the drum with the stick or ruler.

3. Experiment with the size of the tin, and how tight the skin is, to make different sounds.

PROJECT

Make a bottle organ.

You will need:
*a set of matching glass bottles
(8 if possible)
some water.*

1. Fill each bottle with water to a different height.

2. Blow across the top of each bottle.

3. Try to make part of a musical scale by adjusting the water level in each bottle.

4. Arrange the bottles in order. Those with the highest notes go at one end, and the lowest at the other.

What do you notice about the water levels in this order?

PROJECT

Make a stringed instrument.

You will need:

an empty cardboard tissue box

some different-sized rubber bands

two sticks or pieces of wood, about the width of the box.

1. Stretch the rubber bands the long way around the box, making sure they rest over the hole in the box.

2. Place the sticks or wood under the rubber bands near the edge of the box.

3. Pluck the rubber bands with your fingers.

PROJECT

Make a percussion string of bells and cymbals.

You will need:

a pole (such as a broom handle)
a selection of metal objects, for example, saucepan lids, metal cups, forks and spoons, bells
some string
a wooden spoon.

1. Balance the pole between two chairs. Tie the metal objects to the pole with the string.

2. Hit or tap the metal objects with the wooden spoon.

Experiment with the type of sounds you can make.

Why not ask your friends to help with your **orchestra**? Try inventing some tunes.

USES OF SOUND

Being face to face with someone is not the only way to talk to them. How many times a day do you or your family use the telephone?

DID YOU KNOW?

Did you know that 'tele' is the Greek word that means 'far off'?

telephone
television
telescope
telegraph

The telephone is just one of the forms of **telecommunications** available now. Many types of electronic equipment change sound into electricity. Messages and information can be sent all around the world.

All forms of telecommunications need three things. These are: a **transmitter**, or means of sending the information; something to carry the signals; and a receiver to change signals back into something that we understand.

The telephone was invented by scientist Alexander Graham Bell in 1876. This has probably done more to improve communications than any other invention in the world.

When you speak into a telephone receiver, a microphone turns your speech into electrical signals. These are sent via the central telephone company, to the person at the other end of the line. Their receiver turns the signals back into sounds.

The telephone is now in use almost everywhere in the world. The invention of mobile phones means you no longer have to use a telephone inside a building. Communications **satellites** that orbit Earth can receive telephone signals from one country and then beam them back down instantly to another country.

It is now possible to talk to your friends and family in almost every corner of the world.

GLOSSARY

decibel unit used to measure the loudness of
a sound

fluid flowing substance, usually a liquid

hearing aid device to help deaf people hear

insulation material that muffles sound

orchestra group of musical instruments

particles tiny parts of a substance

pitch property of a sound that makes it either
high or low

prey animal that is hunted and eaten by other animals

satellite unmanned spacecraft in orbit around Earth

telecommunications communication of sounds,
signals or pictures over a distance. Telephones,
radio and television are all examples of
telecommunications.

transmitter device that sends out sounds

vacuum space in which there are no particles

vibrate quick back-and-forth movement

volume loudness of a sound

FURTHER INFORMATION

BOOKS

Light and Sound, John Clark (Red Kite Books, 2001)

Light and Sound, Steve Parker (Hodder Wayland, 2000)

Science all around me: Light and Sound, Karen Bryant-Mole (Heinemann Library, 1997)

Science Experiments with Sound, Sally Aston (Franklin Watts, 1999)

Sound and Music, Malcolm Dixon (Evans Brothers, 1998)

Why should I turn the Volume down? and other questions about looking after your eyes and ears, Louise Spilsbury (Heinemann Library, 2003)

WEBSITES

Explore Science – access a library of information on many science topics. Includes photos and artwork, video and animation, activities and tests. http://www.heinemannexplore.com

NOVA Online – faster than sound – read about breaking the sound barrier, discover what creates a sonic boom and find out about recent attempts to beat speed records on land, water and in the air. http://www.pbs.org/wgbh/nova/barrier

Sounds of the World's Animals – learn how people spell and say animal sounds all over the world, and how they're different from one language to another. http://www.georgetown.edu/cball/animals

Speed of Sound Calculator – find out how fast sound travels. http://www.measure.demon.co.uk/Acoustics_Software/speed.html

INDEX

Titles in the Discovering Science series include:

Hardback   1 844 21566 0

Hardback   1 844 21567 9

Hardback   1 844 21568 7

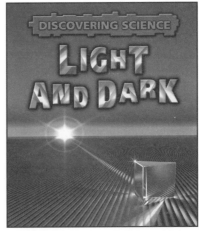

Hardback   1 844 21569 5

Hardback   1 844 21570 9

Hardback   1 844 21571 7

Find out about the other titles in this series on our website www.raintreepublishers.co.uk